A Guide to Life

A Poetic Account of The Spiritual and Material Path

Written & Illustrated by
Samantha Jenkins

A Guide to Life
A Poetic Account of The Spiritual and Material Path

Copyright © 2013 by Samantha Jenkins

Written and illustrated by Samantha Jenkins
www.thesoulstudio.co.uk

Book design by www.pigstydesign.com
Author Photograph by Tina Baker

ISBN-13: 978-1475184150
ISBN-10: 1475184158

Contents

Preface

I was nineteen years old on my first working day as a nursing aide. Before I was introduced to anyone I was told to sit with an older man who was dying. He was lying in bed distressed, calling out for Jesus to 'take' him. I sat by his bedside frightened, not knowing what to do other than hold his hand.

Each day in that job thereafter I helped to feed, wash, dress, and toilet older people, and sometimes I helped layout their dead bodies.

In my early twenties I became an occupational therapist so had countless more encounters with suffering, ageing, dying and death. As time passed I began to feel an inner unease that slowly intensified over the years: a sense of urgency to do something significant with my life; frustration at the banality of my days; a fear of death; and sometimes a fear of life.

Only now, some twenty years on from being a nursing aide, do I understand that this was the beginnings of my spiritual journey and search for meaning in life. A journey that's taken me through the depths of loneliness, fear, confusion and despair, and the highs of inspiration, wonder, peace and joy. A search in which I have invested my time, energy, money, heart and soul.

This book brings together much of my learning from those many years, the personal and professional, the informal and formal, but how I came to write it was quite unexpected. I'd resigned from my part-time post as a University lecturer to try and satisfy my desire to serve, inspire, and bring about positive change, whilst also honoring my values, passions and strengths. Two months on, I suddenly awoke in the middle of one night with some vivid ideas at the forefront of my mind. They didn't make much sense, but I felt compelled to get out of bed and write them down. The same thing happened again the next night, and then the next. By that third night I had a theory about life, which I thought centered on Self-discovery, but as I began to write, the words created this poetic guide to the spiritual and material paths of life. Why do I tell you this? Simply because I feel a need to honor how this book came to be.

You will find that this short guide explores some complex and profound themes, which I trust you will want to revisit over time. Following the introduction, there are two illustrations mapping life's journey along the spiritual and material path respectively, with each then explained in the pages that follow: the spiritual path is headed in pink text, and the material path in blue. You can either compare the two paths page-by-page, or follow them one at a time. Lastly, there is an explanation of how and why these two paths co-exist in life.

To clarify, I am not simply suggesting that the spiritual path is all 'good' and the material path is all 'bad', but that we *suffer* when we focus only on the material path, as we neglect the immaterial reality of our spiritual nature and needs. The spiritual path helps us to re-connect with Source, our true Self, and life itself, enabling us to more fully realize our potential for love, peace, health, and joy in everyday material life. However, I also recognize the spiritual path as somewhat of a developmental ideal to which we aspire, both in the moments and over the course of our lifetime.

Of course, ultimately, only you can decide what is real and important. All I hope is that this book is of service: whether it inspires, challenges, illuminates or comforts you, may it serve you and your life's journey well.

This book comes from my heart and soul

I hope it will reach and touch yours

Introduction

This life is but a transient gift,

yours only for a while.

Given to you

and ultimately cared for by your own hands,

it needs attention,

as you and time march on

with the footprint of your days weaving to create

your life's path,

intentionally or not.

So it is wise to journey with awareness

of your ongoing location and direction,

as there is not only one way for you

to be, do, and live.

Yet so easy is it to be swept

like a leaf in the winds of time,

dormant as you travel

reacting to forces

pushing and pulling you along.

And all the time, time is ticking
by until the end of your road,
when it is too late to recover lost steps
no matter how deep the pain of regret,
there is no going back.
Treasure then
that for now you create your own journey,
each moment, each day
you determine the way.

Still life can be most difficult
to travel
with few signposts along the trail.
So herein lies a guide
to those paths we all tread,
words for you to contemplate,
perhaps a compass to navigate
as you choose
your life, your way.

A Choice
of Paths

Map of the Spiritual Path:
Connection to the True Self

Self: True

Guide: The Source

Energy: Spirit

Health: Promoted

Feelings: Explored

Becoming: More

Quality of Being: Wealth

Everyday: Living

Map of the Material Path:
Attachment to a Created Self

Self: Created

Guide: Society & Ego

Energy: Willpower

Health: Impacted

Feelings: Ignored

Becoming: Less

Quality of Being: Poverty

Everyday: Existence

Explaining the Paths

Guide: The Source

A Mystery

greater than your Self.

A universal, eternal life force

and Source of all,

named God, the Divine, the Creator and more.

A pure flow of creative energy, wisdom and grace

that shines as Light

within and beyond,

awaiting an invitation

to provide you

with guidance, sanctuary, love, peace and hope.

Faith and trust show the way

Guide: Society

Your family, friends, teachers, colleagues and acquaintances,

your environments, culture, history and experiences,

the media, politics, belief systems and norms,

the rights and wrongs and benchmarks

and more and more and more

provide a constant stream of messages

to advise and to guide you,

inform and protect you.

But these can also misdirect, harm or neglect you

unintentionally,

or not.

Who is your Shepherd, and how do they guide you?

Guide: Ego

A facet of your mind that comes to inform you

about reality, adapt you to society

and defend you from pain,

as all alone you meet the world.

Ego employs weapons of thought

like control, praise, criticism and comparison

of your Self, life and others,

and constantly seeks things

like achievement, security, attention and acceptance

as part of its mission

to keep you safe.

Ego fears that you and your life are never enough

Self: True

Your immaterial, essential essence.

Your divine and sacred soul.

Your original and unique nature, passions and gifts,

all compasses to meaning

and purpose in life.

A facet of and resonating with the Source,

be it love, truth, beauty, creativity,

wonder, wisdom, peace or joy,

you are that.

A diamond Light

given to be received in the world.

You were born to be your true Self

Self: Created

Your self-image

weaved over time by ego from various threads

of messages received

about who you must be and must not be

and what you must do and must not do

to be safe, accepted and loved.

Your true colours replaced

with an outline

drawn from opinions, fears, expectations and needs

of others,

to which you grow attached.

How true is your self-portrait?

Energy: Spirit

Your breath of life that flows from Source

as your vital creative life force,

illuminating and animating

your being

so you might express and share

your true Self in the world.

Felt as discernible energy,

spirit invigorates you with a sense

of inspiration, enthusiasm, passion and joy

and soothes you with a sense

of intuitive wisdom, union and peace.

Trust the vital energy of your spirit

Energy: Willpower

Concentrated mental or physical energy

directed towards a life problem or goal,

often used with motivational tools

brandished by your own or another's hand,

like discipline, coaxing, goading, reward or punishment

to push, drive, drag or force you on.

Determined

to override resistance,

willpower can ignore, dismiss and reject

cries from the heart.

In pain to gain.

Power is delicate and easily lost

Feelings: Explored

Feelings experienced deep inside

echo truths

about you and your experiences of life

and help to create

your reality, inside and out.

Feelings are allowed to be

heard and explored with compassion,

given space for mindful expression

and trusted as the way to true love

and connection

with all that is.

Feel your feelings

Feelings: Ignored

The mind presides over the heart

in the belief it's more reliable and true,

critiquing and overriding feeling

to protect you

from personal or public abuse, disorder, or shame

that can come from allowing feelings

both difficult and good.

But feelings ignored or denied

don't always disappear but hide

in thought and behaviour

then misunderstood.

Why trust thought more than feeling?

Quality of Being: Wealth

A feeling of abundance in the heart

of your very existence.

A sense of inner harmony, beauty, rightness, peace,

vitality, love, connection, meaning and joy:

true riches

that flower from the Source of your soul.

A wealth unearthed in relating to and sharing

your true Self,

with time and space to fully be

present in the present,

where all is one.

What greater wealth might there be?

Quality of Being: Poverty

A feeling of loss and lack in the heart

of your very existence.

A sense of inner emptiness, loneliness, longing and pain,

emerging from soul-disconnection.

An internal poverty that propagates hardship

and difficult feelings

towards your Self, life and others,

further compounded by the flame of blame,

it prevents you from seeing the Light:

your Light that burns

a hole inside.

Of all the ways to be poor, a poverty of being hurts most

Everyday: Living

Life offers you precious time

to connect with, rejoice in and share

the full brilliance of your true Self

and to discover and experience each day

is filled with potential

wonder, beauty, meaning, peace, joy, and love.

You have been given a gift

to fully live

and to serve and be served by

all that is

in reciprocal cycles of gain.

Live the present of every day

Everyday: Existence

Attached to a self-created

you exist as a reflection of whoever that is,

spending your time being and doing

all you must, could or should

in response to ego's concerns

with how you appear

and what 'they' might say.

You wait, work for, or forget better tomorrows,

ignoring any façade, grind, or pain of today,

telling your Self it will all be okay

when…

When is the right time to live this one life as a gift?

Becoming: More

In living as a reflection of your true Self

the seeds of your real possibility grow,

as you expand to become more

of all that you are

and ever were

deep in your soul.

For you are already more than enough:

you are precious, radiant, sacred and divine.

Allow your Light to surface

so the world might see your full brilliance

shine.

Why become other than you are?

Becoming: Less

In living as an inaccurate version of your Self

you can deny all you were born to become,

as in action and inaction you move

away from your true core

along ego-driven paths

of approval, excuses, conformity, avoidance,

superiority, rebellion, escapism and more.

Paths that meander from your past

into your present,

influencing your evolution

as you step.

Do you notice where you head as you tread?

Health: Promoted

As you honour and express your true Self

and the energy of your spirit and feelings,

as you have faith and trust

in all that lies within and beyond

and allow your Self to flow with life

you develop a wealth of being,

that is true medicine

to heal, soothe, nurture and fuel

body, spirit, mind and soul,

promoting health

like nothing else.

True health benefits all

Health: Impacted

The neglect of your true Self

is a bereavement felt

as sorrow rising over time,

whilst dormant energies of spirit and feelings

slowly ferment and stagnate,

inducing dis-ease, tension and pain

that grows difficult to numb and ignore.

Vital signs of life

slowly diminish and die,

with a poverty of being created

first inside, then out.

Tend to your true Self

Co-existence
of the Paths

We are born with the essence of our true Self

and the creative life force of spirit within.

A unique blueprint

of our individual nature, passions and gifts,

blended with the universal qualities of soul

like love, truth, beauty, compassion, peace and joy,

all gifted from the Source,

waiting for nurture, love and care

to unfurl and expand

as we grow.

Our feelings are then bestowed

to help shepherd us along our way

in line with the Light

of our true Self,

which comes to illuminate our world

inside and out,

so our gift of life

becomes a gift in life

and we fully experience living

a life that is filled with wealth.

We come to feel abundance in the heart

of our very being

in communion with all that is,

with wonder, meaning, peace and joy found

in fully being

present in the present of each day.

Our briefest moment lived

as an expression of our universal right to be

spirited, creative, playful, powerful, loving, thriving,

alive.

But for many of us as we grow,

worldly messages seen and heard

gradually overlay and decay

the delicate bud of connection to truths in our soul,

as society starts to translate

what our nature, passions, feelings and gifts

really say

about us,

feeding us facts and labels

fished from a historical pool.

We are this, when we do that.

We are like this, but not like that.

We should do this, instead of that.

And so on, and so forth.

Until in time we learn

to translate and ignore

our spirit, nature, passions, feelings and gifts,

that slowly feel poor

foundations for us

to relate to and trust.

Society continues then to cultivate

our mind,

with rational thought, judgement and intellect

prized as reliable and true,

helping us travel the material path,

which we all come to do.

A path focused on external, physical reality,

material beauty, wealth, and success,

a path that can lead us to see these as keys

to lasting happiness.

And we are taught how to be

and taught what to do

and taught what we need to have and become

in unending life lessons from

cradle to grave,

all sifted and absorbed by our ego,

which gradually grows independent

as our protector and guide

with the defences and willpower

to ensure we survive.

Ego creates a self-portrait

to which we attach,

a security blanket wrapped in our mind,

that distorts and morphs our sense

of connection to the unique and universal

qualities of our soul.

And our creative spirit weeps

as we exist as a shadow

of our true Self, with our brilliant Light

trapped inside.

And as we are lost to our Self

we are lost in and to the world,

leading to poverty

in the heart of our very being

that creates holes of suffering, dis-ease and pain

in the variegated threads

of our tapestry of life,

which the material,

no matter how much or how great,

can never fully repair or compensate.

The way then is the spiritual path,

which traverses our inner and immaterial world

on a course that continually spirals,

as we recover and evolve

our sense

of connection with all that is

radiant, sacred, true and Divine,

gravitating ever-closer to the Source

of our Light

whose loving wisdom shines.

A Light that comes to illuminate

darkness and awaken us to see

the infinite gifts and potential

housed in the very heart and soul

of our humanity,

and serving as our guide

as we journey towards the universal doorways

to love, joy and peace,

which will forever release

from inside.

The material and spiritual paths

are not separate then,

they are delicately intertwined

with each influencing and affirming the other

throughout the course of time,

and in treading both

together we will come to find

a way to true harmony

in and between

life and humankind.

No need to reject the created-self,

the material, society, ego or rational mind,

as these serve us

with the means, skill and willpower

to adapt and to survive,

but by also having faith and trust

in the immaterial reality within

we can more fully realize

the meaning of all

it is to wholly live.

We re-connect with the Source

of our true Self, with our creative spirit,

nature, passions, feelings and gifts,

and uncover our own path

to a wealth of being

in material life:

giving and receiving

true abundance

in becoming and shining

our spiritual Light.

This way our whole world expands and gains,

as no-one ever journeys alone.

Each moment, each day

we all co-create the way

life is experienced

and comes to evolve,

and you will serve most when you choose to

be and live true

to all that is true within,

with the ever-present moment *the* opportunity

for you to

begin.

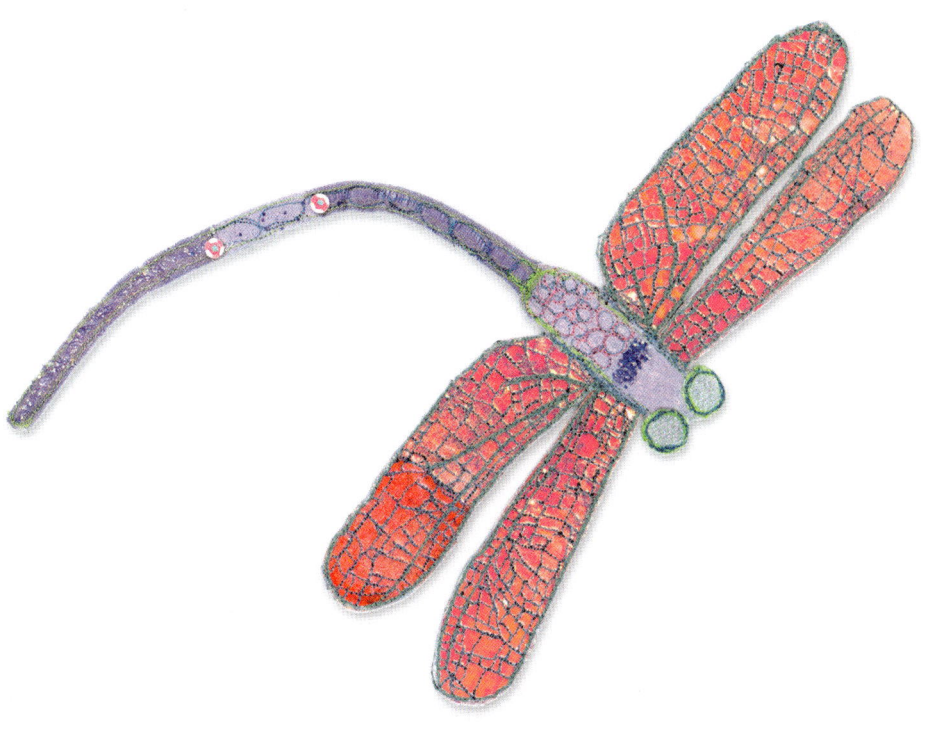

Do not let your life pass you by.

Hold it in the palm of your hands

and nurture it until it blooms

your true colours.

Notes for My Journey

Notes for My Journey

Notes for My Journey

Notes for My Journey

53917162R00042

Made in the USA
Charleston, SC
21 March 2016